MW01382487

GARLANDS & FESTIVE DECORATIONS

Text: Cheryl Owen; Ming Veevers-Carter; Jane Newdick; Jane McDonnell;
Mary Hamlyn; Annette Claxton
Photography: Steve Tanner; Neil Sutherland
Editorial: Laura Potts
Design: Amanda Sedge, The Design Works
Photographic Direction: Nigel Duffield; Mary Hamlyn; Roger Hyde
Illustrations: Phil Gorton; Geoff Denney Associates; Richard Hawke
Production: Ruth Arthur; Sally Connolly; Neil Randles; Jonathan Tickner
Director of Production: Gerald Hughes

CLB 4328
Published by Grange Books
an imprint of Grange Books PLC,
The Grange, Grange Yard, London, SE1 3AG.
© 1995 CLB Publishing
Godalming, Surrey, England.
All rights reserved.
Printed and bound in Singapore.
Published in 1995
ISBN 1-85627-625-2

CREATIVE

GARLANDS & FESTIVE DECORATIONS

Grange
BOOKS

INTRODUCTION

Though most of the arrangements in this book can be made without the need for expensive specialist equipment, some investment in tools will pay dividends. A good pair of scissors are essential, as are a pair of secateurs and a sharp knife. A glue gun, which can be used to glue all kinds of items onto wreaths, baskets, wood and fabric, is also a useful tool. A selection of stem wires, including 18 and 22 gauge wire and silver florist's wire, is also necessary.

TECHNIQUES
Wiring Dried Material
Cut the stems to the required length, usually between 12.5-17.5 cm (5-7 in). Hold the stems together tightly at the bottom between the thumb and forefinger. Bend a wire about two thirds of the way along its length to form a loop. Place the loop under the bunch and hold in place with the third finger. Firmly twist the longer portion of the wire 5 or 6 times around the bunch, making sure that it is secure without being so tight that it breaks the stems.

Binding Stem Wires
Tightly wind stem binding tape twice around the top of a wired stem or bunch to cover the wire. Then, holding the tape at right angles to the wire and pulling it slightly to keep it taught begin to cover the wire. Twist the wire rather than the tape, making sure that the tape overlaps slightly.

Decorative Bows

To make a single bow with tails, make a loop in the ribbon on either side of your thumb and forefinger leaving a similar length of hanging ribbon on either side as tails. To make a double bow proceed as for a single bow but make 2 loops either side instead of one. Cut the ribbon and twist one end of a 22 gauge stem wire around the middle. Cut a small length of ribbon and tie around the middle to cover the wire.

Fabric Bows

Cut a strip of fabric four times the required width and fold in half lengthways. Fold in half again, bringing the raw long edges to meet the fold, and glue. Cut the short ends diagonally, turn under the raw edges and glue. Make a bow with or without tails. To make the 'knot', cut a narrow length of fabric and with the reverse facing, fold the raw long edges into the middle, overlap and glue. Tie around the middle of the bow and cut off excess, or use this to form tails. Use the glue sparingly so that it does not seep through the fabric.

Mounting Candles

If using chunky beeswax candles, simply insert two or three pieces of cane into the bottom of the candle by not more than 2.5cm (1in). Attach legs to other thick candles by cutting 10-cm (4-in) pieces of cane. Hold one piece against the side of the candle and bind onto the candle with green adhesive tape. Then add the next 'leg' and bind as before. When all legs are in place, bind all together a few more times to secure. Legs can be attached to narrow candles, but candle holders are more practical.

PAPER FLOWERS
Making Paper Flowers

Combined with natural dried material such as grasses or used simply on their own paper flowers make stylish arrangements.

To Make the Flower Centre

Bend the end of a length of wire into a hook. Wrap a small ball of cotton wool around the hook. Cut a circle of yellow crepe paper 2.5 cm (1 in) in diameter for the daisies and the buttercups, and a circle of green tissue paper 4 cm ($1^1/_2$ in) for the poppies. Wrap the circle of paper over the cotton wool and glue the circumference to the wire.

Buttercup

Make the flower centre following the instructions given. Cut a strip of yellow tissue paper 4 x 1 cm ($1^1/_2$ x $^3/_8$ in). Cut a fringe along one long side, ending 4 mm ($^3/_{16}$ in) from the opposite edge. Cut the ends of the fringe diagonally to make points. Spread glue along the lower edge and bind around the flower centre. Then stick 2 layers of yellow tissue paper together using spray glue and cut 6 petals using the template provided (page 44). Gently stretch the crepe paper petals widthways. Glue the petals around the flower centre.

Daisy

Make the flower centre following the instructions given. Then using the template provided (page 44) cut a daisy from white crepe paper. Make a hole in the centre. Dab glue sparingly onto the underside of the flower centre and insert the wire down through the hole. Push the daisies up against the flower centre and ensure that is firmly secured.

Poppy

Make the flower centre following the instructions given. Cut a strip of black crepe paper 7.5 x 3.5 cm (3 x $1^{1}/_{2}$ in). Cut a fringe along one long edge, ending 4 mm ($^{3}/_{16}$in) from the opposite edge. Cut the ends of the fringe diagonally to make points. Spread glue along the lower edge and bind around the flower centre. Cut 6 petals from the red crepe paper, using the templates provided (page 42). Gently stretch the crepe paper petals widthways. Glue the petals around the flower centre.

Daisy and Buttercup Garland

Wild grasses are combined with paper daisies and buttercups to make a delightful garland, which is reminiscent of a spring meadow.

YOU WILL NEED:

Dry foam ring • Selection green grasses, wheat, oats • Cotton wool • 18 gauge wire
Yellow crepe paper • Yellow tissue paper • White crepe paper

INSTRUCTIONS

1. Make 20 buttercups using the instructions provided (page 10/11).

2. Make 20 daisies using the instructions provided (page 10/11).

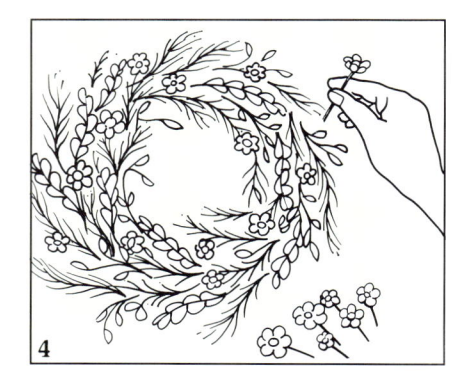

3. Push the stems of the green grasses, wheat and oats into a dry foam ring, all facing the same direction. Ensure that the foam ring is well covered and that the edges are completely hidden.

4. Arrange the paper buttercups and daisies in the wreath at random creating a balanced effect.

Valentine Wreath

Bring a touch of romance to a wedding reception or an anniversary celebration with this heart-shaped wall decoration.

YOU WILL NEED:
2 bunches Ageratum • 100 stems dried red roses •18 gauge wire • Silver wire

INSTRUCTIONS

1. Use silver wire to join two 18 gauge wires together and bind with stem binding tape (page 8/9). Attach ends together by forming a loop and hook. Bend wire to form a heart shape.
2. Wire rose heads singly with silver wires and cover with stem binding tape (page 8/9). Wire Ageratum into groups of 5 heads and bind.
3. Twist flowers onto heart starting from the middle top and working outwards and downwards. Try to keep the flowers even all the way around. It is important when wiring the flowers to the wreath to rest the heart on a work surface, as this will make working easier.

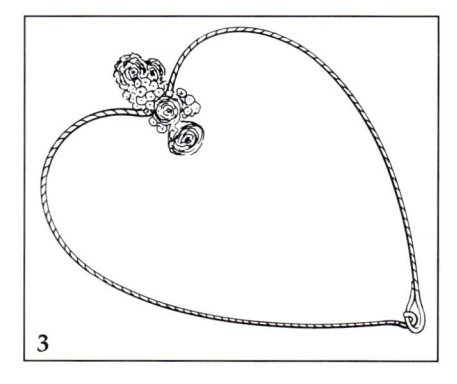

Spring Wreath

This vibrant decoration, made using painted paper leaves, will brighten your home all year round.

YOU WILL NEED:
Dry foam ring • Watercolour paper • Watercolour paint • Stem wire Tape • Artificial berries

INSTRUCTIONS

1. Cut leaves from watercolour paper using the spring and autumn leaves templates provided (page 42) and the virginia creeper templates (page 43).
2. Dampen the leaves, then paint a pale shade with watercolour paint. Before the paint dries, paint a slightly darker shade at the base, blending the colour upwards. Try to ensure that the leaves are slightly different shades of colour.
3. Paint 'veins' on the leaves in a darker shade with a fine paintbrush. Fold the leaves along the veins.
4. Tape a length of wire to the back of the motif with the wire extending downwards from the shape.
5. Gloss varnish the leaves.
6. Push the leaves into a dry foam ring, placing them in the same direction.
7. Add small bunches of artificial berries, pushing the stems into the ring at regular intervals.

SCENTED SUMMER GARLAND

Golden marjoram leaves give a sweet, herbal scent to this colourful garland made from marigolds and nasturtiums.

YOU WILL NEED:

Oasis ring • Marigolds • Nasturtiums • Alchemilla molis • Golden marjoram leaves 18 gauge wire • Florist's tape

INSTRUCTIONS

1. Soak the foam ring base, following the manufacturers instructions where applicable. Cover the 18 gauge wire with stem binding tape (page 8/9) and twist onto the wreath. The wire ring should be tight enough so that it does not slide easily around the ring.

2. Cover the whole ring with foliage and filler until the foam is hidden. Take particular care to cover the edges of the ring.

3. Add the marigold flowers throughout, spacing them evenly round the ring.

4. Add the nasturtiums and other smaller flowers in a more random

pattern, building up the arrangement until the whole appears well balanced.

TRADITIONAL COUNTRY WREATH

Geranium flowers, sweet pea, green sedium and stokesia are combined in this wreath to capture the very essence of summer.

YOU WILL NEED:

Oasis ring • Alchemilla molis • Geranium • Sweet pea • Green sedium • Stokesia

INSTRUCTIONS

1. Soak the foam base in a large bowl or sink, following the manufacturers' instructions where applicable.
2. Cut stems short on the Alchemilla molis so that you have plenty. Use them to cover the foam, creating the background for the finished arrangement.

3

3. Add the small flower heads and other materials, mixing the blooms well and scattering them evenly through the arrangement. Make sure the inner edges of the ring are well hidden, adding further blooms where necessary.

HARVEST GARLAND WITH POPPIES

Natural cereal grasses have been combined with brilliant red paper poppies to make a stylish autumnal wreath.

YOU WILL NEED:

Dry foam wreath • Selection dried grasses, wheat and barley • Cotton wool
18 gauge wire • Green tissue paper • Black crepe paper • Red crepe paper
Florist's tape

INSTRUCTIONS

1. Make 7 poppies using the instructions provided (page 10/11).
2. Push the stems of the grasses, wheat and barley into a dry foam ring, positioning them in the same direction.
3. Push the poppy stems into the wreath at regular intervals, using them to add depth to the arrangement.

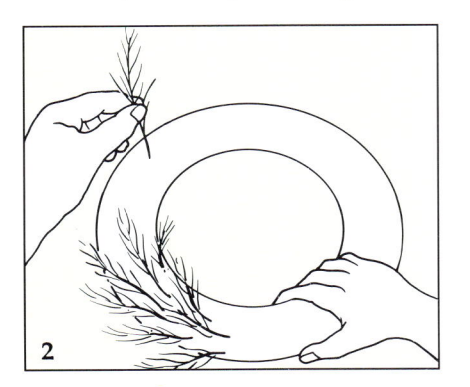

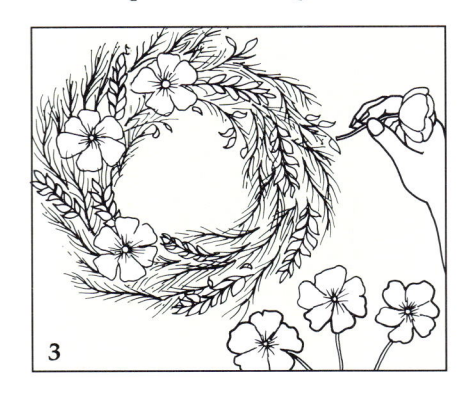

CHRYSANTHEMUM WREATH

This beautiful wreath is made with fresh flowers and makes a stunning table decoration. The dark green foliage serves as the perfect foil for the russet red of the flowers.

YOU WILL NEED:

*Oasis ring • Woody stemmed foliage (including sweet box and waxflower)
White spray carnations • Peach spray carnations • Russet red spray chrysanthemums
Button chrysanthemums*

INSTRUCTIONS

1. Soak a green oasis ring in water, following the manufacturers' instructions where applicable. Dry the plastic base with a cloth and place the wreath in a good working position. Cut short sprigs of about 5 cm (2 in) long of foliage, including sweet box and waxflower. Place the sprigs evenly around the wreath covering as much of the base as possible.

2. Cut the stems of the white and peach spray carnations, including the buds, to match the height of the foliage. Place these evenly around the wreath so that no large spaces are left.

3. Add the focal flowers of russet red spray chrysanthemums and button chrysanthemums, balancing the colours and shapes evenly around the wreath. Give the flowers a final light spray with water to keep them fresh.

AUTUMNAL GARLAND

This rustic garland combines fir cones and painted paper leaves to great effect, making a long-lasting arrangement.

YOU WILL NEED:
*Dry foam ring • Watercolour paper • Watercolour paint • 18 gauge wires • Tape
Small fir cones*

INSTRUCTIONS

1. Cut the leaves from watercolour paper using the spring and autumn leaves templates provided (page 42), the virginia creeper templates (page 43) and the ivy leaf templates (page 45).
2. Dampen the leaves, then paint a pale shade with watercolour paint. Before the paint dries, paint a slightly darker shade at the base, blending the colour upwards. Ensure that the leaves are varied in colour, ranging from brown, red, orange, and ochre.
3. Paint 'veins' on the leaves in a darker shade with a fine paintbrush. Fold the leaves along the veins.
4. Tape a length of wire to the back of the motif with the wire extending

downwards from the shape.
5. Gloss varnish some of the leaves, leaving the others plain. This will give the finished wreath variety.

6. Push the leaves into a dry foam ring, ensuring that they are all facing in the same direction. Make sure that the foam base is well covered, and that the edges are well hidden.

7. Wire the small pine cones. To do this circle an 18 gauge wire around the base of each cone, making sure that it is caught between the scales. Twist the ends of the wire to secure.

8. Push the cones into the ring at intervals in small groups.

CHRISTMAS WREATH

This dramatic door wreath, made with an unusual selection of dried materials, is a delightful way to welcome Christmas guests to your home.

YOU WILL NEED:

Twig wreath 35 cm (14 in) in diameter • Assorted dried cones
Assorted artificial and dried fruits • Walnuts • 3 dried corn cobs
1 m (1¹/₈ yd) ribbon • 18 gauge wire • Florist's tape

INSTRUCTIONS

1. Cover the 18 gauge wire with florist's tape (page 8/9) and twist onto the wreath. The wire ring should be tight enough so that it does not slide easily around the ring. Leave the ends of the wire apart so that they can be twisted into a hook once the wreath is completed.

2. Apply a line of glue from a glue gun down the length of the corn cobs. Attach at intervals to the wreath.

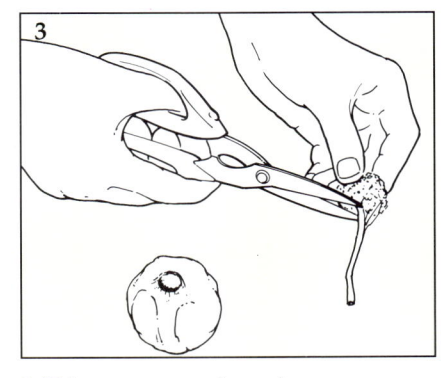

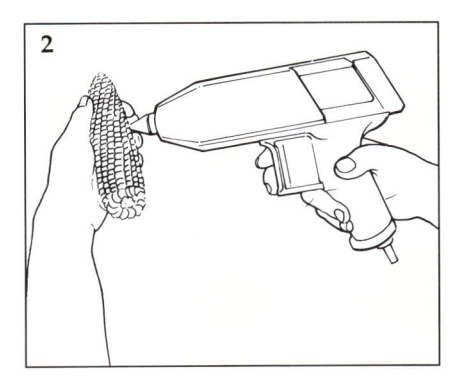

3. Trim any stems from the pomegranates and other artificial and dried fruits as close to the fruit as possible. Glue the larger items to the wreath. Fill in any gaps with the small items until the wreath is full and chunky, making sure that the overall effect is well balanced. Leave 2.5 cm (1 in) of the ring bare for a ribbon bow.

4. Make a large double-looped bow (page 8/9) and attach to the wreath.

ANEMONE AND CHRYSANTHEMUM SWAG

Light and fresh, this floral swag makes the perfect decoration for a buffet table, particularly for a special occasion.

YOU WILL NEED:

Chicken wire • String • Sphagnum moss • Wire ties • Eucalyptus • Senecio Asparagus fern • White chrysanthemums • Gypsophila Purple and blue anemones • Freesias

INSTRUCTIONS

1. Measure the length of your intended swag with a piece of string. Cut a piece of chicken wire about 30 cm (12 in) deep using the piece of string to measure the required length.
2. Tease out the sphagnum moss and spread it in the middle along the length of the chicken wire.
3. Roll the chicken wire over and secure the ends with wire ties. Squeeze the roll into a sausage shape to use as the base of the swag.
4. Cover the swag base with eucalyptus, senecio and asparagus fern.

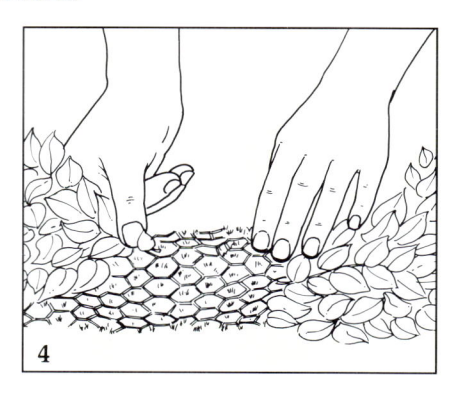

5. Add the white chrysanthemums and gypsophila, spreading them evenly through the arrangement.

6. Add the feature flowers of purple and blue anemones and freesias, concentrating them towards the centre of the swag to ensure the whole arrangement is well balanced. It is important to make sure that the flower heads tilt up slightly towards the top of the swag so that you can see them from eye level when the swag is placed in position on the table.

Vine Leaf Garland

This attractive paper garland makes an unusual decoration for a celebration table and can be painted to complement the colour scheme of the table that it is adorning.

YOU WILL NEED:

18 gauge wire • Florist's tape • Cotton pulp balls • Pink paint
1 sheet dark green paper • 1 sheet light green paper • Gold spray paint • String

INSTRUCTIONS

1. Cover stem wires with stem binding tape (page 8/9). Push cotton pulp balls onto the lengths of covered wire. Paint the balls and then push them into a dry foam block covered with paper to allow them to dry.

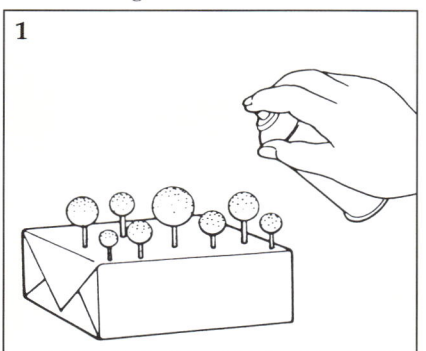

2. Cut vine leaves from 2 shades of green paper, using the templates provided (page 44). Fold the leaves down the centre and along the 'veins'.

3. Spray the balls and leaves lightly with gold paint.

4. Tape a length of wire to the back of the motif with the wire extending downwards from the shape.

5. Cut a length of string to the required length. Bind four or five leaves to it with florist's tape. Then attach two or three berries to the bunch with florist's tape. Continue adding the leaves and the berries in this way until the swag is the required length.

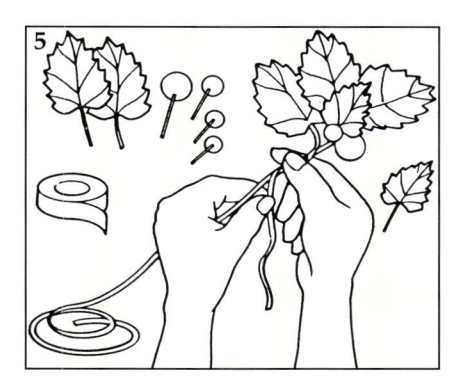

Yuletide Swag

Made from evergreen foliage and decorated with bows and baubles, this traditional Christmas swag brings a festive air to the buffet table.

YOU WILL NEED:
Chicken wire • String • Sphagnum moss • Wire ties • Evergreen foliage (fir or yew) Baubles • Stem wire

INSTRUCTIONS

1. Measure the length of your intended swag with a piece of string. Cut a piece of chicken wire about 30 cm (12 in) deep using the piece of string to measure the required length.

2. Tease out the sphagnum moss and spread it in the middle along the length of the chicken wire.

3. Roll the chicken wire over and secure the ends with wire ties. Squeeze the roll into a sausage shape to use as the base of the swag.

4. Cover the swag with evergreen foliage such as yew or fir, tucking the stems in firmly and working outwards towards the ends.

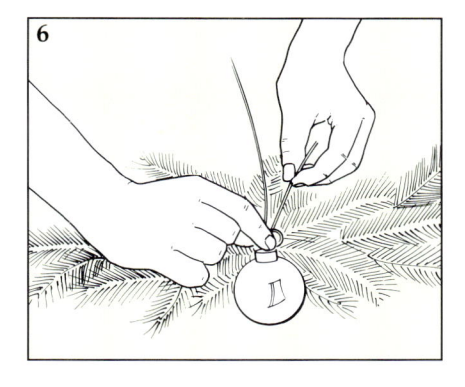

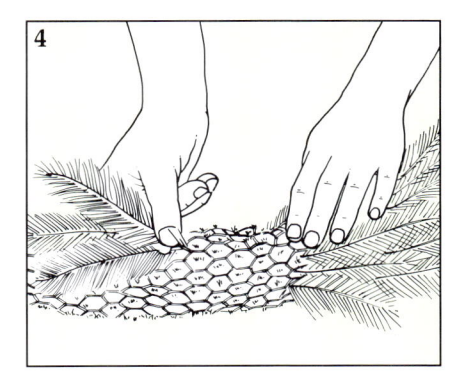

5. Make two bows using gold coloured florist's wired ribbon (page 8/9). Wire these onto the swag.

6. Wire red, gold, bronze and clear shiny Christmas tree baubles, threading the wire through the metal hoop at the top of the bauble. Push the wires firmly into the sphagnum moss, spreading them evenly along the swag.

CANDLE ARRANGEMENT WITH POINSETTIA

Red poinsettia has been combined with sweet box and fir in this festive candle wreath.

YOU WILL NEED:

Oasis ring • 4 plastic candle holders • 4 candles • Evergreen foliage Poinsettia

INSTRUCTIONS

1. Soak a green oasis wreath shape, following the manufacturers' instructions where applicable. Dry it with a cloth. Push four plastic candle-holders into the wreath.

2. Cover the wreath with evergreen foliage, using sweet box and fir, pulling it over the edges to hide the plastic base. If the wreath is only to last for a short time add green poinsettia leaves.

3. Place red poinsettia bracts around the wreath. Place red candles in the four holders.

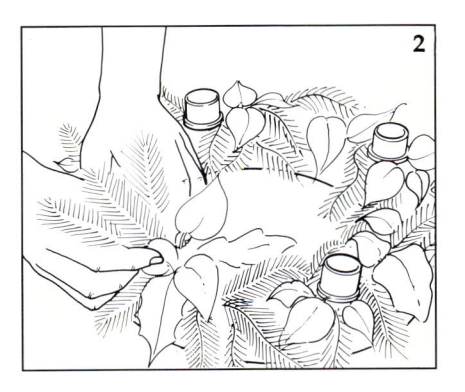

Beeswax Candle Table Decoration

Beeswax candles give off a sweet, honey-like scent when lit, making this arrangement the perfect centrepiece for a festive table.

YOU WILL NEED:
Dry foam block • Florist's tape • 2 green canes • 2 large beeswax candles
18 gauge wire • 22 gauge wire • Walnuts • 25 assorted cones • Gold spray paint

INSTRUCTIONS

1. Cut the block of foam in half to make a shallow, full-width piece. Place on a black tray and cover lightly with moss.
2. Tape the foam and moss in place. Cut 2 green canes into 6 pieces. Insert 3 pieces into the bottom of each candle, making sure that they do not stick in more than 2.5 cm (1 in).

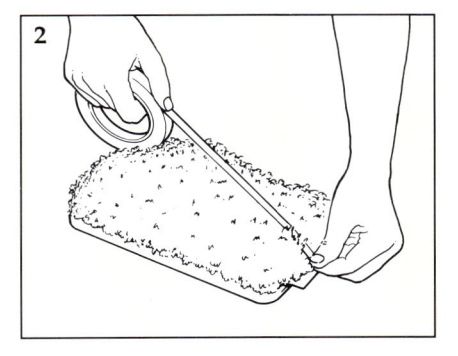

3. Spray one half of the cones lightly with gold paint. Wire the cones, using 22 gauge wires for small and medium-sized cones and 18 gauge wires for larger cones. Circle the wire around the base of the cone making sure that it is caught between the scales and twisting the ends together tightly to secure.

4. Mount the walnuts onto wire, dipping the end of a 22 gauge wire into latex-based adhesive, and pushing it into the nut base where the two halves join. Leave to dry.

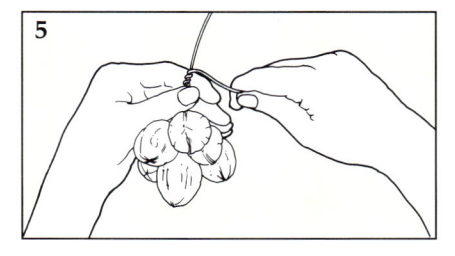

5. Make 11 bunches of walnuts, grouping them together in groups of 5. To do this bend a wire about two thirds of the way along its length to form a loop. Place the loop under the group of five wires and twist the longer portion of the wire 5 or 6 times round the bunch.
6. Begin the arrangement by inserting the two beeswax candles into the foam, making sure that they are secure. Build up the arrangement with the bunches of walnuts and the fir cones, until a full, well-balanced effect has been achieved.

Festive Fruit Basket

*A magnificent combination of colours and textures,
this decorative basket makes an eye-catching display.*

YOU WILL NEED:

*Wicker basket • 18 gauge wire • 22 gauge wire • Gold spray paint • 5 bunches large
cinnamon sticks. • 20 assorted cones • 1 m (1⅛ yd) fabric • 1 m (1⅛ yd) ribbon*

INSTRUCTIONS

1. Attach fabric to the basket rim at 15 cm (6 in) intervals with 22 gauge wires.

2. Wire bunches of cinnamon together. To do this put two or three in your

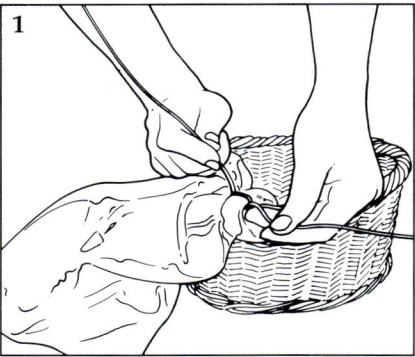

hand and roll them so that they fit together quite closely. Then wind a wire around the centre, so that it is tight enough to cut into the bark slightly, and twist the ends together to secure.

3. Mount the cones onto 18 gauge wires. Circle the wire around the base of the cone making sure that it is caught between the scales and twisting the ends together tightly to secure. Spray the cones lightly with gold paint.

4. Attach cinnamon bundles and cones to basket rim with wire 'stems'. Trim excess wires. Tie ribbon around each cinnamon bundle to cover wire.

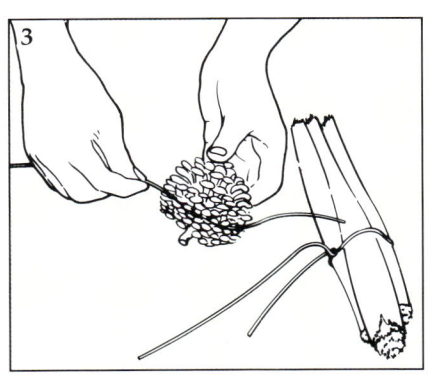

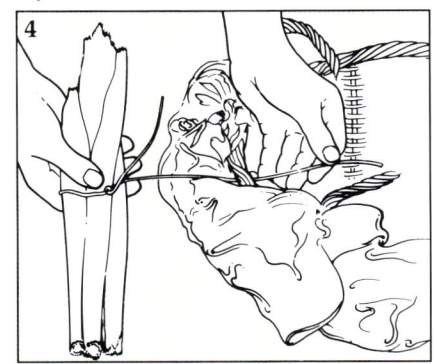

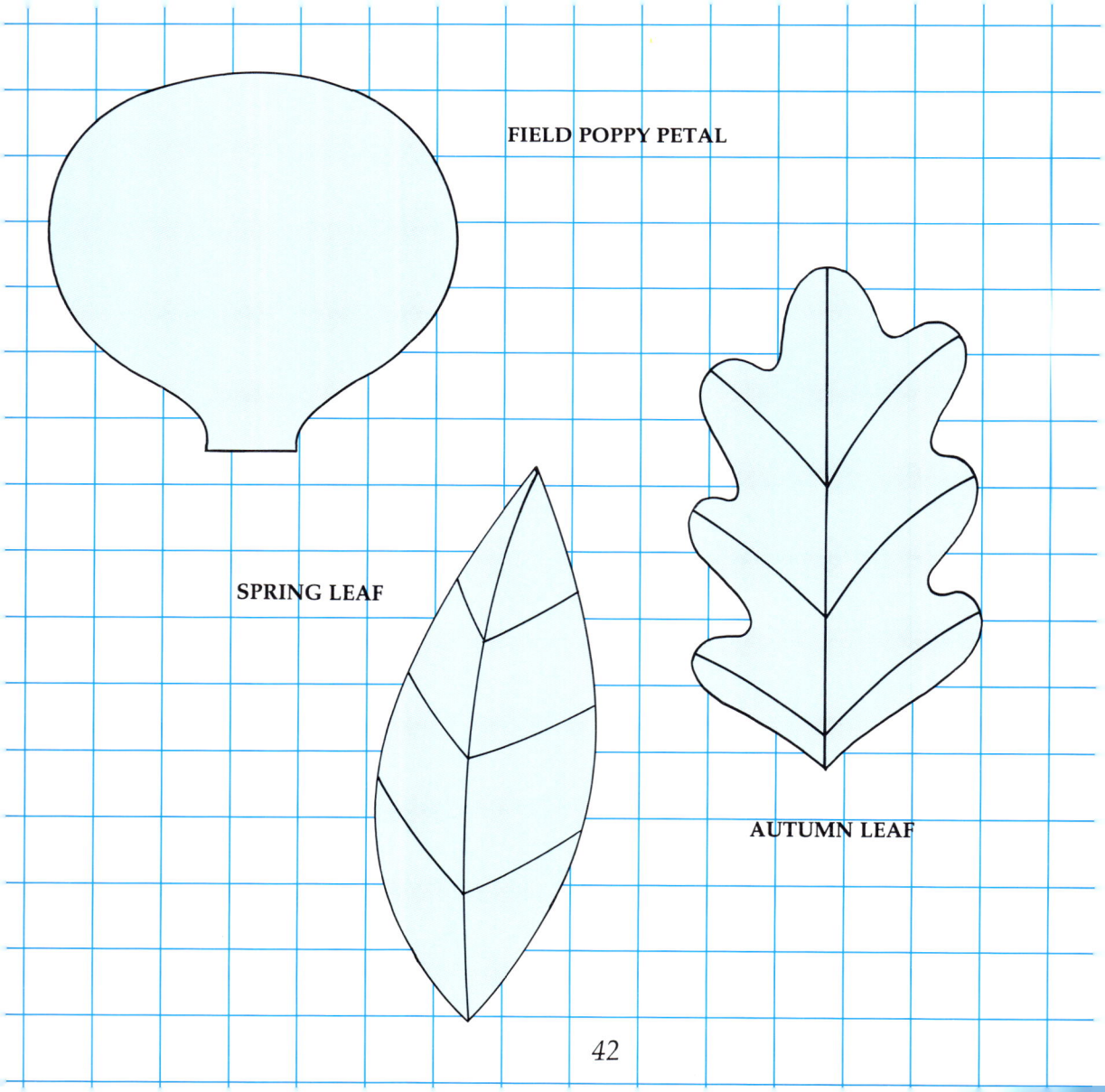

FIELD POPPY PETAL

SPRING LEAF

AUTUMN LEAF

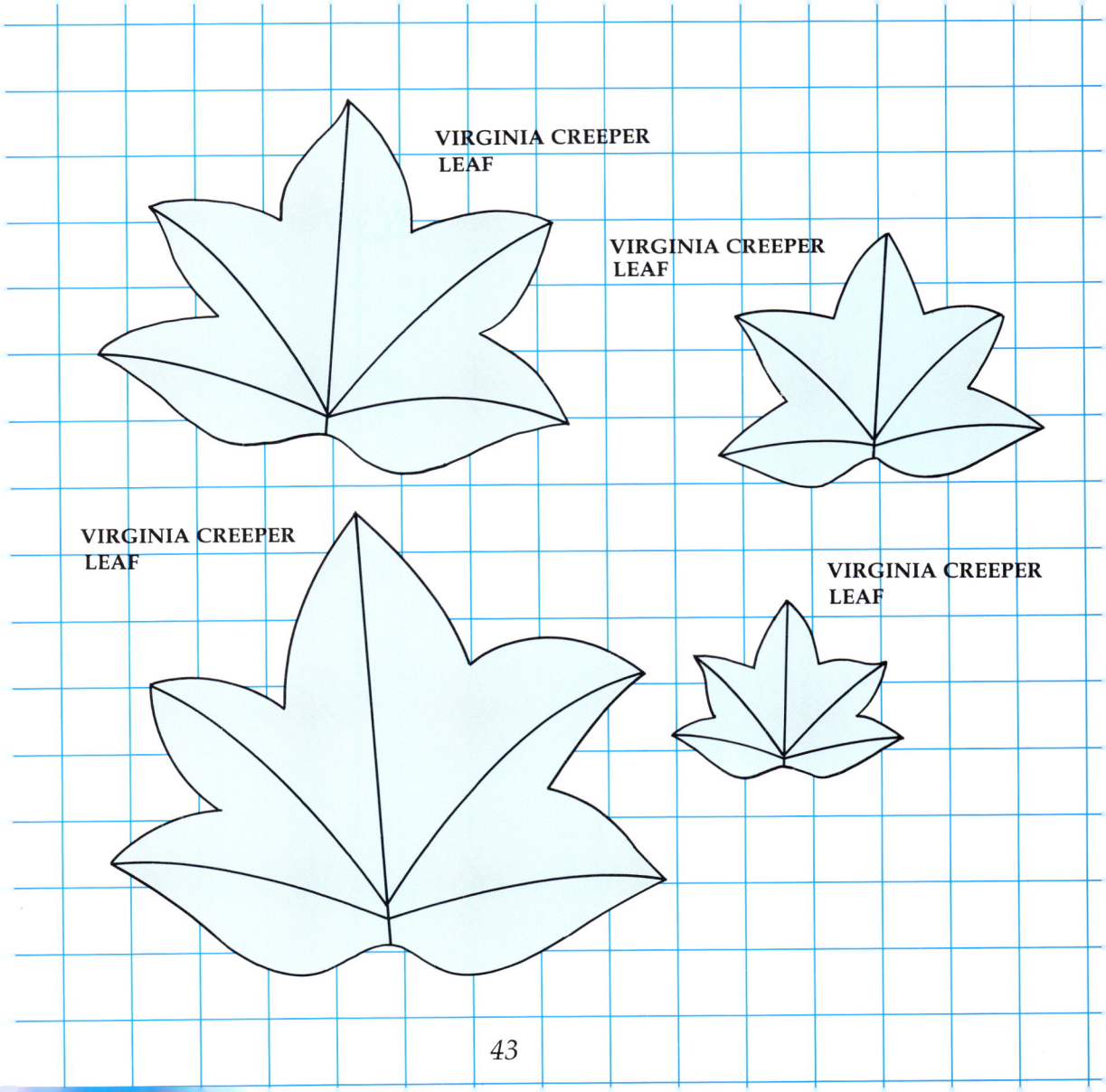

VIRGINIA CREEPER LEAF

VIRGINIA CREEPER LEAF

VIRGINIA CREEPER LEAF

VIRGINIA CREEPER LEAF

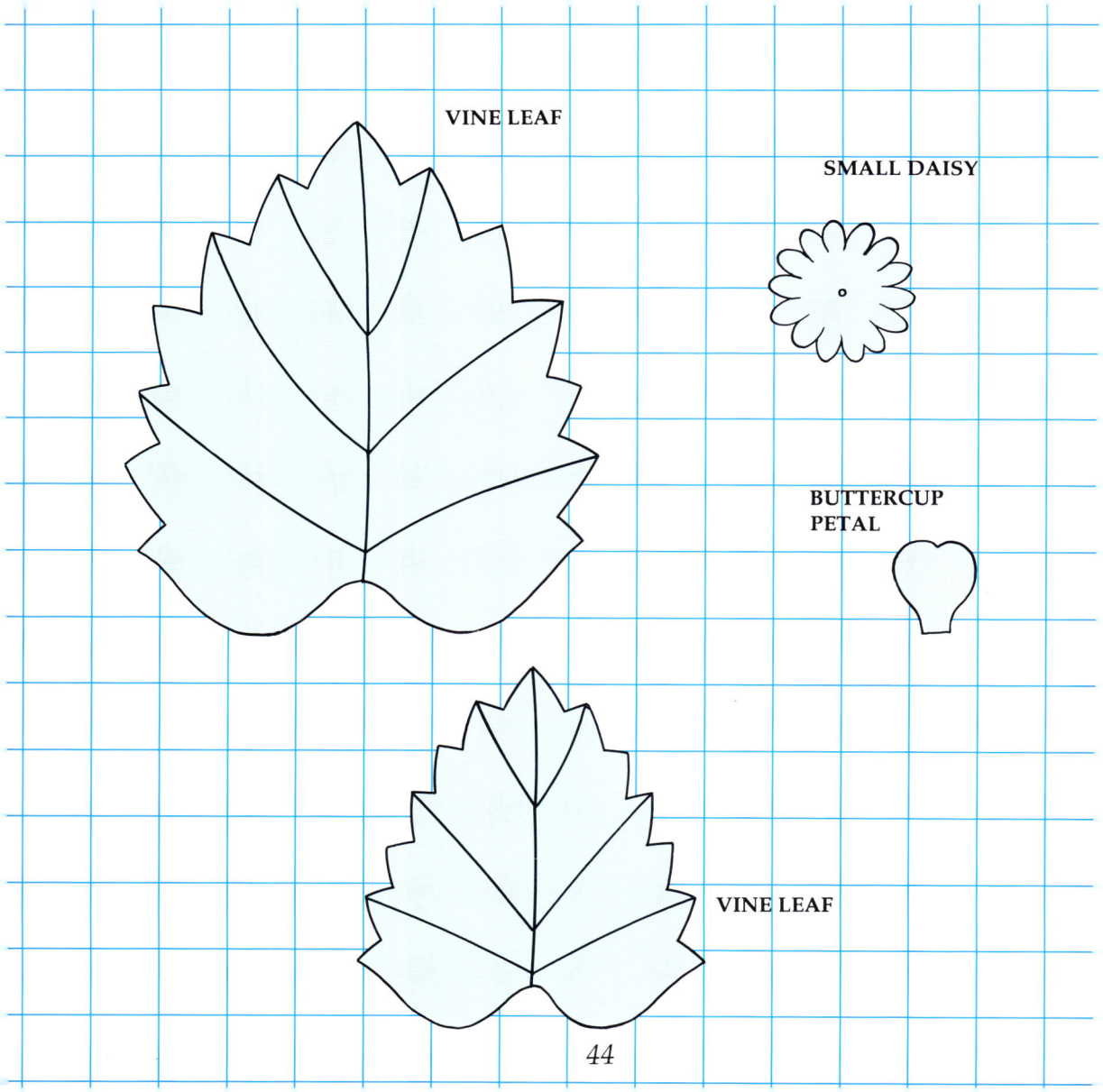

VINE LEAF

SMALL DAISY

BUTTERCUP PETAL

VINE LEAF

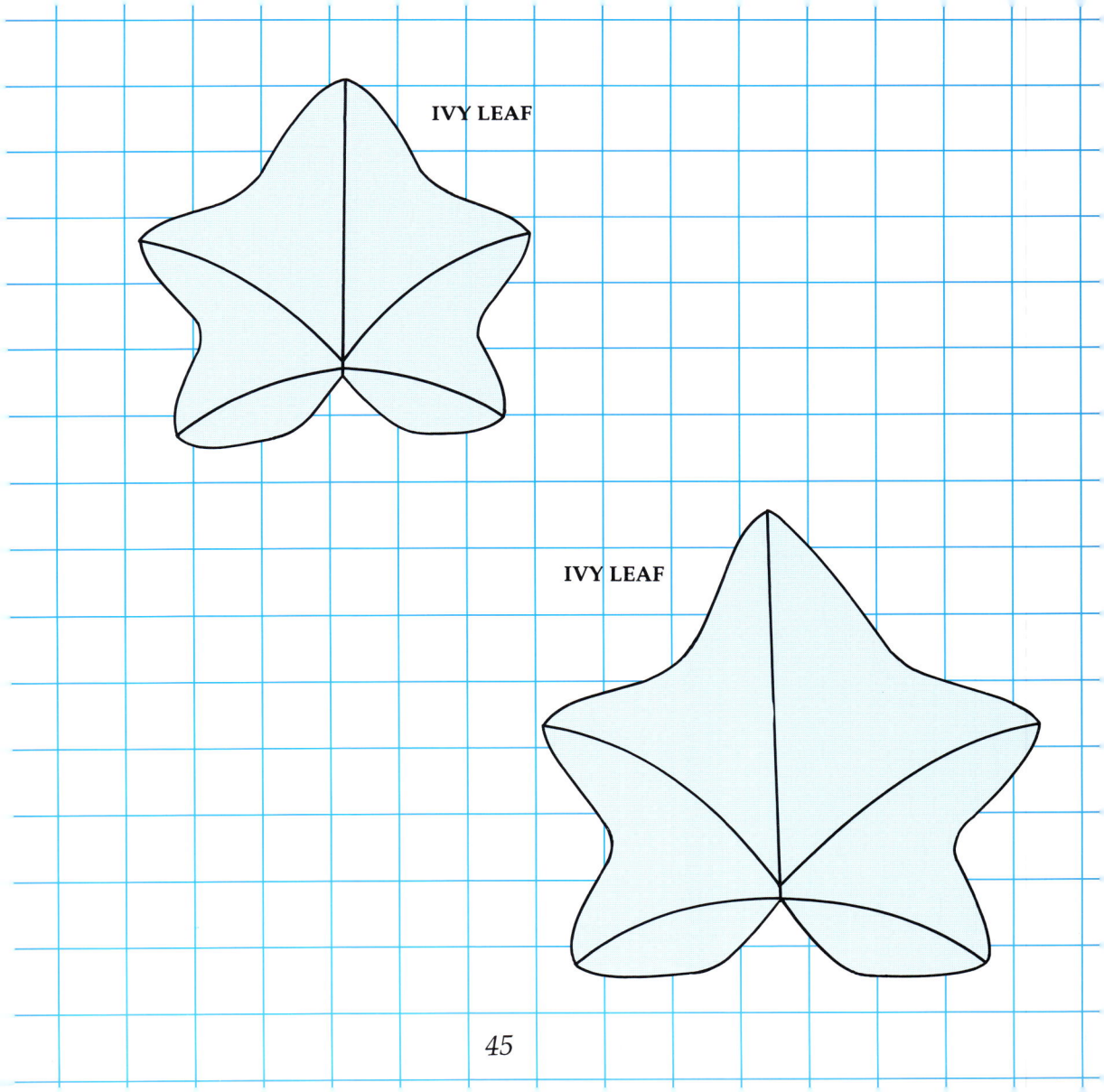

IVY LEAF

IVY LEAF